'It is possible for unimaginable futures to become true. Set your fears aside, dive in and follow this indispensable 'do earth' strategy. Tamsin is relentless in presenting the convincing message of climate and ecological emergency with a valuable set of tools for any of us eager to soften our footprint on earth. And Tamsin's personal experience and storytelling makes it so much more than a mere guide. I will no doubt find myself turning instinctively to the advice Tamsin provides all of us to create a future beyond the limits of our imagination.'
Dr Achala C. Abeysinghe, Country Representative for Papua New Guinea, Global Green Growth Institute

'It is so easy to feel powerless in the face of the climate and ecological emergency, but this book is a true awakening — a call to arms. The stakes have never been higher. *Do Earth* makes you fall in love with our planet once again. I urge you to find time for it; you won't regret it.'
Alice Aedy, photographer & co-founder, Earthrise Studio

'Tamsin encourages us to stay hopeful by sharing inspiring stories from their organising and gently reminding us that we can learn through reconnecting with the earth as individuals and as a community. Crucially, they equip us with the important tools we need to resist the fatalism that plagues so many of us in our day-to-day lives.'
Amina Gichinga, organiser with London Renters Union and The Nawi Collective

'Passionate, engaging, visionary but eminently practical, this is a powerful guide to becoming active in the urgent task of healing both the earth and ourselves, from one of the country's most respected and creative campaigners.'
Caroline Lucas, MP for Brighton Pavilion

'A delightful handbook that viscerally connects the reader with their inner activist; unlocking knowledge, inspiration and practical tools to help transition our society toward a better future. There is love in the words of this book. A warrior spirit that is filled with the magic of our communal home, and the gifts you can have if you spend a little time building a relationship between yourself and the earth.'
Arizona Muse, model & activist

'Beautifully written, Tamsin's journey from despair about climate change to healing our inner and outer worlds as one (because they are), takes you lovingly by the hand and invites you to join the collective path. A testament of the mind and a song of the heart.'
Christiana Figueres, Former Executive Secretary of the UN Framework Convention on Climate Change and architect of the Paris Agreement

'Tamsin guides the reader through what we humans face in the coming years, offering knowledge and tips so that we can take appropriate action. I hope this book will be the beginning of a path for friends we've yet to meet so that we can find our strength and stand with each other in the fight for all of life.'
Clare Farrell, co-founder of Extinction Rebellion

'Reading Tamsin's book felt like having my heart held and given warmth. It is a brilliant road map to help us heal ourselves and our planet; a book filled with genius analysis and earth-saving tips. Go read it now.'
Daisy Lowe

'Tamsin's book is so warm, compassionate, courageous, practical and bursting with love and life. It's not just a handbook for activism but also a way to live. Tamsin's wisdom and insight into practical matters, such as how to structure meetings and foster community, is totally brilliant and feels like a guide for cutting-edge organisations right now at this moment in time.'
Ed O'Brien, Radiohead

'Many of us will be spending the rest of our lives working towards creating a fair and liveable future. This brilliant book works as a guide to nurture ourselves through the times we live in. It's easy-to-read, yet provides a beautiful depth and clarity.'
Fay Milton, musician (Savages) and co-founder of Music Declares Emergency

'An honest and unflinching look at where we are now, and where we need to head. It perfectly captures Tamsin's approach to activism championing love, hope, optimism and resilience, whilst providing a pragmatic plan of how to move forward. If you read one book on climate change this year, make it this one.'
Jack Harries, co-founder, Earthrise Studio

'This how-to book by a brilliant Green activist gently takes the reader on an important journey. Alongside Tamsin, we learn about the problems our planet faces, discover why we should care and learn what we can do to preserve the earth — through letting go of the practices that are damaging it.'
Baroness Jones of Moulsecoomb

For seekers, dreamers and doers;
for all who know peace in nature.

Tamsin Omond

Do Earth

Healing strategies for humankind.

Published by
The Do Book Company 2021
Works in Progress Publishing Ltd
thedobook.co

Text © Tamsin Omond 2021
Photography © Alice Aedy 2021
p12 © Jim Marsden
p17 © Adam Murphy/Alamy Stock Photo
p72, p96 © Tamsin Omond
p93 © Miranda West
p128 © Moana Ghiandoni

To find out more about our company,
books and authors, please visit
thedobook.co or follow us **@dobookco**

5 per cent of our proceeds from the sale
of this book is given to The Do Lectures
to help it achieve its aim of making
positive change: **thedolectures.com**

Cover designed by James Victore
Book designed and set by Ratiotype

Printed and bound by OZGraf Print
on Munken, an FSC® certified paper

MIX
Paper from
responsible sources
FSC
www.fsc.org   FSC® C163799

A CIP catalogue record for this book
is available from the British Library

ISBN 978-1-914168-00-0

10 9 8 7 6 5 4 3 2

Contents

Prologue: From a field in Wales to a rush
   on Parliament   13

Introduction: You don't have to be perfect
   to care about the earth   18

Part One: Self

1. How bad is it really?   34
2. I'm just one person   44
3. What's stopping us?   52

Start here: 5 ways to soften your footprint
   on the earth   59

Part Two: Community

4. Together we stand   64
5. My neighbourhood   72
6. What does winning feel like?   86

How a small group can make a place better   91

Part Three: Earth

7. The hollow tree   96
8. How to fall in love with the earth   100
9. Quiet the mind and notice miracles   108

Afterword: I promise   120

Resources   126
About the Author   129
Thanks   130
Index   132

**Dreams and reality are opposites.
Action synthesizes them.**

—

Assata Shakur

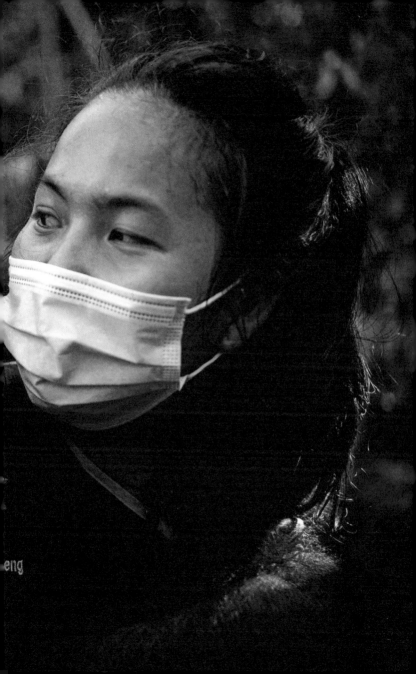

Prologue

From a field in Wales to a rush on Parliament

The Do Lectures, which are the inspiration for these
Do Books, began in 2008 on a farm in the Welsh countryside.
I was invited to lecture at the first gathering. One year out
of university, I was working for Greenpeace and helping to
organise grassroots environmental activism. The invitation
from 'Do' was the first time I'd been invited to talk about
a big idea. Until then, public speaking had been limited to
planning media strategy at protest camps or explaining
climate change to communities in meetings near
Heathrow Airport.

I arrived at the first Do Lectures via a train from
Paddington Station. Sat by the window I snuggled into
the grey leather and plush green pillows of Great Western
Railways train décor. Since there had never been a Do
Lectures event before, I had no idea what to expect but
as we pulled out of the station my imagination was full
up with the open-hearted influence of Paddington Bear,
the promised escape of the railways and — as I looked
around the train carriage — an understanding that this
was the start of an adventure.

I changed train three times and at each more remote
station, a woman who'd been sat near me since London
ran with me to catch the connecting train. We'd both been

scribbling in notepads with headphones in our ears but in the final hour of our five-hour journey I caught her eye for a moment and grinned. Our smiles caught us both by surprise. I asked where she was going and discovered we were both guests of the Do Lectures. I was going to speak about how non-violent direct action — like the suffragettes' law-breaking — can turbo-charge social change movements and she was going to write about the lectures in her column for the *Sunday Times*.

A man in a minivan met us from the train. We were the latest arrivals to a group of the variously bewildered; people who had travelled across the country to meet outside this train station nestled in Welsh hills. Bespectacled men with fleeces and duffel bags were the other lecture givers. We threw our luggage into the back of the van and everyone piled in. We drove at speed along single-track roads. We'd reach the top of a hill and gasp as the van flew forward. It was late summer; the light was slowly dying and drenched the countryside in gold. When we arrived, we were directed to tents and told to prepare for dinner.

I walked into the hall where we were going to eat and saw grown-ups, at ease with their success. The only thing of note I'd done was to get arrested for dropping banners protesting Heathrow Airport's third runway from the roof of the Houses of Parliament. I didn't know anyone and I felt ill at ease.

Amelia Gregory, who I'd seen on stage calling ceilidhs in Finsbury Town Hall, waved at me. She ran *Amelia's Magazine* and we'd met a couple of times at protests that she was covering for her blog. She made space on the bench next to her and I squeezed in.

'You're in the programme! What are you talking about?'

On 13 October 1908, thousands of suffragettes met in Parliament Square. A handful of them pushed through police lines and rushed towards Parliament. None of them got in, but the violence of the police response and the disobedience of these women made the suffragette cause front-page news. I had an idea to celebrate the centenary of the 'Suffragettes' Rush' by organising something I was calling Climate Rush.

'It will be a bit like the suffragette rush, but about climate change.'

'Then everyone should dress up as suffragettes,' Amelia said.

Two brothers — Ben and Dan — were listening. They were at the Do Lectures to make a film about the event.

'You'd *try* to get arrested?' They didn't look convinced.

'Controversial protest makes climate change less academic. People write about it. They get emotionally provoked and because of that they think about what's happening, they talk about it with their friends. They have opinions on it.'

John Grant — the guru of green advertising — who had been quietly eating, looked up. 'That's what you should talk about in your lecture.'

Four months later, on 14 October 2008, I was released from being held overnight at Horseferry Road Magistrates' Court. When I came out of the building the brothers who'd been filming the Do Lectures were both there, documenting the story of Climate Rush. Amelia was too. We'd been working together every day since the Do Lectures. Her idea that everyone should dress up as suffragettes was the foundation of a Climate Rush that captured creative imaginations. She passed me a cutting from the *Sunday Times*. There was a picture of us rushing at Parliament dressed as suffragettes. Jessie, the journalist I'd been on the train with, had written about us.

Just a handful of months after sharing the idea of the event, we had formed a group and attracted a crowd more than a thousand strong. Led by Caroline Lucas (now the Green Party MP for Brighton Pavilion), we broke through police lines and rushed Parliament. We surrounded the Palace of Westminster that night, forcing MPs to stay in the main chamber and listen to the chants of 'Climate Action Now'.

Throughout my journey I've drawn strength from remembering how Climate Rush began. As an idea in my head it wasn't going to do anything. It became something tangible and powerful when other people decided to get involved. At that point, it became so much better than anything I could have made happen alone. Remembering this teaches me something that I'm still wrapping my head around. We can't do anything alone, it's the alliances we form and the ways we find to work together that changes the world, and us.

You don't have
to be perfect
to care about
the earth

You only have to let the soft animal of your body love what it loves.

Mary Oliver, 'Wild Geese'

This book is about learning from nature. It's about letting go of practices that harm our planet and making different choices for our lives. Writing it has been a celebration of all the magic that exists outside my front door and the people whose ways of doing life enrich my own. Before we begin I want to lift up the wisdom of Indigenous people who offer us a planet that is alive and sacred. How we begin to learn from their perspective is everything this book will explore.

I'm a white non-binary person from a comfortable background who has always lived in London. I left university not knowing what I wanted to do. The 2008 financial crash had just happened and the promise of 'more' that I'd grown up with seemed shaken. When I heard that, despite climate change, the government was going to expand Heathrow Airport — the biggest single source of greenhouse-gas emissions in the UK — I wanted to do something. I packed a bag and took my tent to join a camp of environmental activists who were occupying the land where the airport hoped to expand, just outside Heathrow's perimeter fence.

I was scared by the science of climate change. As a queer person enjoying freedom and pride, I was scared of how LGBT people would be treated in a world of climate breakdown, I was scared by lessons from history, that when natural disasters, resource wars and economic hardship hits, communities who are marginalised, vulnerable or oppressed become scapegoats. I worried about what would happen to human rights — fragile and recently won — in a world that is bracing against a hostile climate.

I haven't stopped worrying about that, but fear is not my driving force anymore. Although it can be a powerful motivator, the panic fear creates is in opposition to the healing that we need to foster. It's an insecure foundation for environmental activism.

I didn't act out of love of nature and I wasn't interested in learning from the cycles of the earth. Instead, I was breathless, wanting to be the perfect activist; relentless in my efforts to stop climate change by targeting policies and infrastructure that had big greenhouse-gas emissions tied to them.

One decade of activism

The ten years that followed the first Do Lectures I crammed full of activism. Climate Rush wasn't just a single event. We became a group that captured media headlines and got people talking about climate change. We took over Heathrow Terminal One by unfurling picnic blankets and holding an Edwardian picnic dressed as suffragettes. We blocked Westminster Bridge before it was standard protest etiquette to do so and we dumped a load of horse manure on Jeremy Clarkson's drive.

When the coalition government formed and tried to sell off England's public forests, I cornered Rachel Johnson (Boris's younger sister) at a swanky *Evening Standard* do and persuaded her to create a new organisation with me.

Under the title of 'Save England's Forests' we went through her address book and organised a letter that was signed by Dame Judi Dench, Gillian Anderson, Tracy Emin and the Archbishop of Canterbury, to name a few.

Our letter, which declared the privatisation of England's forests to be 'unconscionable', was front-page news, and a petition against the sale leapt from a few thousand signatories to hundreds of thousands. Three weeks later Prime Minister David Cameron announced his government wouldn't be selling off the forests after all.

Always on the lookout for carbon-intensive infrastructure to oppose, I turned my focus to the streets that surround London City Airport. My relationship with Newham — the area of London where the airport is, and where I now live — began when a group of us cut through the perimeter fence and chained ourselves around the wheel of a private jet. We made headlines but when we started knocking on doors to find out what local people thought of the airport's expansion, we quickly realised that its pollution and noise was just one more challenge facing the people who lived there.

Led by the mums in the area, we formed a kids' choir called The Royal Docks Singstars. Whilst the children were singing, parents gathered signatures on petitions against the airport's expansion that we sent to all levels of government. We held a TedxNewham at The Crystal, London's new City Hall, where we celebrated the resilience of a community that wakes up every day to jet-fuel fumes and aircraft noise. Ethel Odiete, one of the mums living there, asked why her community — young, poor and Black — should bear the brunt of living in the shadow of an airport that serves the 1 per cent.

Three decades of delay

All of the activism I've done has tried to influence what we are doing in relation to the earth. Much of that has been based in London, where I live, but I've also been part of the international conversation about how humanity responds to the climate crisis.

These conversations have been taking place every year since 1995. They are held under the United Nations Framework Convention on Climate Change at annual gatherings called COPs. COP is an acronym for 'conference of parties'. The 'parties' are our government representatives from all the nations of the world. The meetings usually happen for two weeks in December and their aim is to create international legislation, plans and programmes to tackle the climate emergency. The annual COPs are the only government-led process that humankind has yet created to get the whole planet, together, to respond to the climate emergency.

Everyone with skin in the game goes to the COP. Alongside representatives of 193 nations and all their advisors are NGOs, charities, faith-leaders and an overkill of delegates who represent powerful polluting industries and fossil-fuel lobbyists. Whilst the nations discuss the measures they might be willing to take, the trillion-dollar corporate interests use all their might to railroad the discussions. As dialogue breaks down inside the conference centre, tens of thousands of activists gather outside to protest an international process that so far has had too little success.

I've been to many COPs since my first in 2009. That one was held in Copenhagen and everyone — even President Obama — was there. A lot of people had pinned their hopes on a legally binding deal emerging from the discussions.

Poor nations, who have historically emitted very little and are now being hit hard by climate impacts, were excluded from the most influential conversations. The entire environmental movement was exhausted and despondent when no deal was reached. For me, a newbie activist protesting loudly outside the convention centre, it was confusing. Why couldn't our elected leaders come together more than once a year to sort this issue out?

We need everyone

It's been more than a decade since my first COP. During that time I have been involved in many environmental campaigns. Throughout my journey there have been the same people and the same voices. Whether it's Greenpeace, David Attenborough or Greta Thunberg, a lot of awareness raising has been done by a relatively small (if impressively loud) group of people.

Their work has provoked millions to prioritise the environment, which—when focused—has led to successful, policy-shifting campaigns. However, we can't allow such a small group of people to carry all our environmental responsibility anymore. They can't change the relationship that each and every person has with the planet. If we want to change the impact that humanity has, it will take each of us doing something different, so wherever you are and whatever you're doing, there's a role for you in this great transformation.

As we approach planetary boundaries that should not be passed—like the melting of the Arctic or the burning of the Amazon—we need much more than the activity of environmentalists to turn our ship around. Now we need everyone.

Earth consciousness

I spent my twenties scared of climate disaster and busy organising. In my early thirties I burnt out from living with zero balance and too much activism. I'd made it my mission to stop climate change. When I realised that heaping it all on me wasn't just impossible but also delusional, I felt like I'd failed at the only thing that gave my life meaning. Since then, I've been slowly putting myself back together and in the process re-evaluating my relationship to activism and to the planet I've been so desperate to 'save'.

It's a funny idea that we who have caused nature so much harm will be the ones to save the planet.[1] It's an idea that makes human success or failure the centre of the story, when we might learn more if we became humble and focused our attention on the earth's strength and resilience. We got into this mess because we dominated nature, forcing it to provide our every consumer want. Instead of care and respect, we extracted until we reached this point of environmental crisis.

We have pushed both our planet and ourselves, ignoring natural limits. Instead of learning from the earth about how to rest, heal and regenerate, we celebrate humankind as separate from and dominating nature. I want to let go of such an arrogant worldview. I want to give up trying to control the natural world and other humans too. Fighting bad policies is part of a new story that is taking root, but to heal we don't just need to fight, we also need to become enchanted by the planet again.

The way nature brings peace to my busy mind feels like one of the most abandoned parts of who I am. Slowly I am

---

1   The global North is responsible for 92 per cent of all CO_2 emissions. Since 1850 we have created and vigorously promoted this way of life as the only viable model for development.

rekindling it. I walk in the woods and I feel at ease. It becomes easy to hear the world whisper, 'This is everything that is happening right now.' Lost beneath the boughs of trees, there's nothing I need and instead I feel healing power between the earth and me.

I read articles about people who talk to plants. Their mental health improves and the data shows their plants grow stronger. I pay attention when I catch sight of a jay's turquoise feather or a blue tit's yellow chest and it feels like a gift. Walking through a forest on a winter's day, the sunlight reflects through tiny droplets of caught, cold water and transforms my path into a lair of delicate jewels. I delight in these things the more that I realise I'm part of them. At an atomic level I belong to nature and Earth's nourishment is written into the coils of my DNA.

This story of belonging with nature is the one I want to return to all my life. It's the beginning of a more sophisticated environmental practice than just loudly saying no. We will still need to turn away from the fossil-fuel era, but when we look to nature's abundance we can feel inspired about what the next phase of human evolution might be.

Tools to scrutinise where we're at

The ultimate hidden truth of the world is that it is something we make. And could just as easily make differently.

—

David Graeber

In this book, I'll introduce ideas to help us think about whether the world we have is the world we want to keep.

I'll share tools that we can use to create different worlds even within the shell of the one we have. I'll talk about being in right relationship: an idea I learnt through reading the work of Black feminist organisers based in the United States. Imagining a right relationship gives us a way to talk about how we want our relationships to be. It helps us to describe what is wrong with the ways of relating we've currently got, so that we can get better at demanding a reality that would feel more 'right'.

Getting in right relationship means noticing things we've been conditioned to ignore and drawing on the power of this new awareness to demand something different. It's about coming closer to who we are when all the pressures or expectations of society are taken away. It's about feeling peace and easy joy in our relationships with the natural world, each other and ourselves. When it comes to the earth, a right relationship begins with the recognition that we are part of nature. We humans aren't separate — we are created, natural beings.

From this acknowledgement that we are part of nature, we might challenge the story that our destruction of earth is inevitable. Even though we have lived out of balance with nature, the idea that it's in our makeup to hurt the earth feels so wrong.

Old excuses for dominating the world

We need to be able to interrogate our relationships and ask whether the patterns of behaviour, in terms of how we treat ourselves, each other and the planet, are healing us or doing us harm. To help us consider these questions, there are three big ideas that we need to become comfortable talking about. They're words that describe how people in

Western culture relate to each other and to the planet. They're useful words because they bring into the light some of the harmful assumptions behind our current way of doing things.

Patriarchy, white supremacy and capitalism are three assumptions about how things should be that have defined our white, Western culture. They're assumptions that have been created and fused throughout our society by those who hold power. Under these assumptions, we accept it as unfortunate but inevitable that humans will treat each other and the planet in oppressive and destructive ways. If we are to heal the earth, ourselves and each other, we need to find strategies to acknowledge and transform these assumptions.

Words like capitalism, white supremacy or patriarchy sound scary and impenetrable, but to change the underlying fabric of our society, we need to understand the fabric that we've currently got. These three ideas are the dominant belief systems of our Western society. They describe how we have been taught to relate to each other. Each one has — at its core — an assumption of dominance, creating a society where some people dominate other people and we all dominate nature. They are a series of hierarchies that keep us busy, desperate to maintain our controlling position, judging ourselves by where we are on these hierarchies — who we get to be better than — and fearing that we may lose this status.

Patriarchy creates a hierarchy of gender and puts cis men at the top. White supremacy creates a hierarchy of race and puts white people at the top. Capitalism creates a hierarchy of value and puts the ability to make profit at the top. Capitalism insists on an economy that extracts profit from everything, rather than building an economy that cares for life and for the planet. It reminds us again and again that we are either more or less than our fellow human beings, rather than giving space to recognise that we are interdependent, co-creating humanity together.

In capitalism, if we aren't producing profit (i.e. making money) then we're not valuable and we don't have worth. This is an exhausting logic. It exhausts me, and the people I love, when we internalise it and believe that if we're not being productive, we have no worth. It's a logic that says the things we love the most — our time, environment and relationships — are only valuable if they are producing profit. It's the logic that values a forest only when it's been logged.

Developing our awareness of these systems that pattern our society takes work. None of us signed up to these categories, we were just born into a society where they powerfully existed and we took our place accordingly. If these hierarchies do continue to be the status quo, then we will continue to pit ourselves against each other and to assume a right to dominate the earth. I really hope that's not the future we choose.

It's going to take time and effort for us to unlearn what we've been taught, but we do now have a choice to change and grow. If we make that choice we will oppose the assumptions behind these hierarchies wherever we find them. As we begin to uncover the ways we've been encouraged to see people and planet as resources that we can dominate and extract profit from, we stand a chance of letting go of these impulses and getting in right relationship.

A road map of where we'll go

Over the course of this book, I'll share with you strategies I have learnt to shift my perspective on these belief systems every day. By doing this I try to be part of other, gentler worlds where healing can happen. These worlds are beginning to exist beyond the limits of patriarchy, white supremacy and capitalism. In these unsung places we are on a level, able to look each other in the eye and do the work that needs to be done.

Wherever you are on this journey, I want to travel some of the road by your side. I want to imagine how it will feel when we let go of fear about our place in the hierarchies and instead relate to each other with abundance, resourcefulness, service, collaboration and trust.

I've divided this book into three sections. It builds from where we are now — *Self* — through what we need — *Community* — in order to heal — *Earth*.

In the first section, *Self*, I'll explore where we are and why we've got caught up in such a mess. I'll share ways that we can make different decisions to soften our footprint on the earth. I'll talk about why we want to do this but also what the limit of such personal lifestyle action is.

In the second section, *Community*, I'll offer guidance on how you can take more collective action and belong in a community. I'll share my experience on how to hold meetings, win campaigns and organise collectively.

In the final section, *Earth*, I'll share earth-conscious practices that give me joy in the everyday. In the world that is coming, we will need greater resilience so in this part of the book I'll offer strategies to kindle your empathy and encourage your optimism regardless of what the changing climate brings. More and more of us are committing to protect the planet, but to show up to that work without it taking enormous toll on our spirits and bodies, we're going to need to foster a culture of compassion, patience and rest.

Our aim is to develop relationships with the earth that heal and nurture more than they harm and extract. It's not going to be easy. There is so much that we need to unlearn if we're to relax and let the world support us.

None of us want to be responsible for a world in ruin and right now that doesn't have to be our legacy. We're an adaptive, resilient and constantly changing species on a constantly changing and regenerative world. As the hurt that we've caused becomes impossible to ignore, we are a species on the crest of taking responsibility.

It's a big moment to be alive because right now, more than ever before, everything we do really counts. Our human species needs to go somewhere drastically different from where we are and that means every choice we make is either taking us towards a different future or cementing ourselves in a way of living that the earth cannot support.

This book is my gentle encouragement — a road map of possible ways to live more earth-consciously. The most important thing is that we try, and that we try again, when we find the road too daunting. You are part of a community now, people who are doing their best to respond. I've written this book because I'm in that community with you: sharing what I've learnt, offering advice and celebrating the gorgeous rest that comes when we nourish self, community and earth.

It may be ten minutes to midnight, but that means we are now six hours away from dawn.

Another world is not only possible, she is on her way. On a quiet day, I can hear her breathing.

—

Arundhati Roy

SELF

1
**How bad
is it really?**

Antonio Gramsci is a social theorist who I learnt about when five friends and I organised a book club. We wanted to understand some of the big ideas that intellectual people talk about so we created a place where we could study together without judgement for what little 'social theory' we knew. One of the ideas that we came across in the first book we read was Gramsci's concept of 'the interregnum'.

In 1930 Gramsci was in prison because Mussolini's fascist government wanted to 'stop his brain from functioning'.[2] Whilst Gramsci was in prison he wrote *Prison Notebooks*, which contain his most culturally influential ideas. Four years into the 20-year sentence, Gramsci wrote, 'the crisis consists precisely in the fact that the old is dying and the new cannot be born; in this interregnum a great variety of diseased symptoms appear'.

When I first read that it struck a chord. It seems like we're living through an interregnum right now. We see and

---

2   That's what the state prosecutor said at Gramsci's trial — Hoare, Quintin; Nowell-Smith, Geoffrey (1971). Introduction. *Selections from the Prison Notebooks*. By Gramsci, Antonio. Hoare, Quintin; Nowell-Smith, Geoffrey (eds.). New York: International Publishers. pp. xvii–xcvi. ISBN 0-7178-0397-X.

feel that there is something wrong with our way of life. We know that we can't keep taking from nature and destroying the world. We think about how we might need to pull together if the human species is going to last and then we worry because there's no clear plan for how to change this world or find other ways of doing life to replace 'the old'.

Everything is changing so fast but instead of getting prepared and learning how to roll with the punches, we dig our heels in and resist. Whether it's climate change, AI, racial justice, a pandemic or mass unemployment, we don't want to acknowledge how uncomfortable it is when the foundations of our civilisation shift beneath our feet. We're scared of these changes and, instead of acknowledging it, we feel overwhelmed and decide that the safest option is to put our heads in the sand. If we keep doing that, we will suffocate.

Like it or not, there are significant changes happening to our planet. There are also systems of power hellbent on maintaining the status quo. The powerful know that the best way to keep their power is by persuading us that the way things are is the way things must remain. They win if we do nothing and in their version of reality, the enormous costs to our way of life are inevitable. A ransacked planet, people oppressed because of their economic situation, class, race, gender or disability and a mental-health epidemic are excused as unfortunate but inevitable consequences of our species' footprint on the earth.

The changing climate is an emergency that has been coming down the road ever since the Industrial Revolution. It's an emergency that collides with our ecological impact, as rampant resource use means that other species and habitats are disappearing fast. Those in power have known about it for over 40 years. They've done so little to prepare us for what's coming. It's time for us to look to each other and become the people we can trust to help us through.

Get comfortable with the facts

There is now no weather we haven't touched, no wilderness immune from our encroaching pressure. The world we once knew is never coming back.

Dr Kate Marvel, climate scientist at NASA Goddard Institute for Space Studies & Columbia Engineering's Department of Applied Physics and Mathematics

Most climate activists have their own go-to scary science fact. Mine is about the melting of the Arctic sea ice. It's the only climate impact that I know a lot about. With this information, I give myself permission to have an opinion on climate change. Instead of worrying that I don't know enough and leaving climate change as a subject for scientists to discuss, I learnt a little so that I feel confident sharing my thoughts and fears.

The Arctic sea ice is melting faster than anyone predicted. This is bad news because the Arctic ice regulates our global temperature. The white ice acts like a refrigerator, cooling the entire planet down. It also reflects the sun's light and heat, which keeps the planet surface cooler. When the summer Arctic sea ice melts for good (predicted to happen between 2035 and 2050), apart from massive sea-level rise and bad news for polar bears, we will lose the refrigerator and sunlight reflector at the top of our planet.

Global heating will increase because the white surface of ice will be replaced by dark-blue ocean that absorbs (rather than reflects) solar energy. No one can make an exact prediction of how bad this will be for escalating climate change. One thing climate scientists do know is that losing the Arctic sea ice will have an unprecedented effect on global temperatures and sea-level rise. It will destabilise the conditions under which our human species thrived.

Move beyond denial

Whilst we would do well not to overwhelm ourselves with bad news, we do need to check in with it from time to time. It keeps fresh in our minds that radical changes to how we live have begun and that more is coming. We don't avoid them by putting our head in the sand. Rather we avoid being hit hard by them if we respond now by staying alert to reality and building lives in preparation for change.

Where the climate and ecological emergency is concerned, we've been a species in denial. It's time for us to get a handle on the situation so that we can begin to face up to just how quickly we need to move. We're in the sixth mass extinction of life on this planet. It's the most rapid in pace and it's the only extinction event to be caused by a single species — the human species. Our planet used to be 99% wildlife and 1% human. Now it is 4% wildlife, 36% human and 60% livestock. We're not going to be able to protect ourselves, or the species we share this planet with, by pretending it's not happening.

Climate change is happening faster than the cautious predictions of past scientific consensus. Globally we aren't prepared for the scale of natural disasters that will happen because of the rising global temperatures on our world.

With the amount of greenhouse gas emissions that we have already produced, global temperatures will increase by 1 degree Celsius (33°F) at least. Even if we stopped burning fossil fuels today, we would still have to refocus our global economies to cope with the amount of climate change that we've already caused.

But we're not going to stop burning fossil fuels today. We have not come close to flattening the curve of greenhouse gas emissions. Instead, emissions keep on rising, with more than half of all the CO_2 emitted since 1751 being emitted in the last 30 years. If we don't bring climate change emissions down radically, we are headed for a world where global temperatures will rise well beyond 2 degrees Celsius (35°F). Google what scientists predict will happen to life on our planet for every additional degree that global temperatures rise. It is scary, and I'm sorry that telling the truth about this is a prerequisite to us taking the actions that I'm exploring with you here.

Don't blame yourself...

Although awareness of the problem and desire for action has never been more widespread, the climate and ecological emergency is not at the top of any political agenda, nor is it the issue that sits in the background, providing context for all our more short-term concerns. It should, because the state of the planet is the context in which we spend every day of our lives. If the earth can't support all the lives we need it to support, then every other issue we care about will take a back seat (or become much worse) as we struggle with each other to survive.

The people who have money and power in this world got there by playing the system. Their wealth and influence is dependent on a world fuelled by oil and gas, where people who put profit ahead of everything else succeed. What that looks like is huge industries such as fast fashion that exist only because they are permitted to destroy the environment, sidestep paltry legislation and mercilessly exploit their workers. It's a world that gives enormous profit to industries that burn hydrocarbons even when we know the cost of that is climate ruin.

Visionary political leadership right now would require people in power to acknowledge how far-reaching the scale of change to our economy, society and culture must be. Our leaders need to find the courage to set us on a path of transformation and to keep us on that path, however difficult it might be. Lamentably, very few leaders yet have that vision and this is partly because the majority of our leaders belong to the same elite that is getting rich from planet-wrecking capitalism.

... or get defensive

None of us like being told that we need to change. It's one of the reasons we're not that keen on activists. We see their actions as criticising us and so we harden against them for telling us how to live.

Many environmental activists (including me) have come from one fairly affluent demographic. It's not particularly appealing to watch white middle-class people tell everyone else to change how they live their lives. However, this model of white people wagging their fingers is what Western countries have been doing on the global stage. Our wealth and development was built on exploiting the earth and the labour of our colonies, and now we say we won't act until the rest of the world promises not to develop.

The best ideas the white Western world can come up with are the systems of power — patriarchy, capitalism and white supremacy — that have backed everyone on the planet into a climate and ecological emergency. Our version of global leadership has brought us to this place where, despite all the stuff we've created, when it comes to protecting the planet, we have failed.

Do become part of the solution

In terms of becoming resilient and sustainable, white Western cultures have the furthest to go. We need to learn from everyone that we have historically oppressed if we're going to weather the coming storms. In this we can borrow the language of North American social movements who talk about organisers rather than activists. Organisers are people who have noticed what is happening and want to do something about it. We roll up our sleeves and get on with it. Organisers can be all of us.

We're choosing to do something because we recognise that either we encounter the new reality well-resourced and prepared or we'll be hit hard by it. We're choosing to act because not acting is beginning to hurt. We want to heal ourselves through healing our relationship with the planet.

Whether it's the insect apocalypse or the melted Arctic, the raging forest fires or the prediction from The Institute for Economics and Peace that the climate crisis could displace 1.2 billion people by 2050, you are essential to building this movement from where it is to where we need to be.

2
I'm just
one person

> Once we start to act, hope is everywhere.
> So instead of looking for hope, look for action.
> Then, and only then, hope will come.

Greta Thunberg

For six months, when I was 31, I lived in Berlin. When I first arrived, I went to meditation meetings. They were a place to make new friends and also to learn coping strategies so that I could recover from a decade of non-stop activism.

Sabina was one of the people I met meditating. She was in her early 50s, dressed in the loose-fitting clothes you'd expect of someone attending a group meditation, and then she challenged that stereotype by wearing a gold-plated grille over her bottom teeth. She asked me how I'd come to Berlin and I took it literally, describing my journey overland by train. Sabina smiled and invited me for tea.

As I got to know her, I realised that Sabina didn't — and still doesn't — drink, smoke, eat meat or consume any animal products. She doesn't fly or own a car and she still uses a Nokia brick owned for 15 years as her mobile phone. She goes to the flea market every weekend and spends hours and a few euros on a treasured piece of fashion. She never speaks about these choices as sacrifices; in fact she never mentions them at all.

I used to collect my eco-conscious ways as an armoury. I took pride in the knowledge that I was making better choices than most people. Sabina is one of the people who helped me to understand how exhausting it is when every choice we make is used as an opportunity to judge everybody else. With Sabina I saw a different way of living in balance with the earth. She just got on with it. Making choices because they made her feel good. Inspiring people with her harmony rather than her martyrdom.

Her actions aren't for show or to make a statement. She just lives lightly in right relationship with the earth. Whatever she is missing out on, she doesn't seem to care because the way she's chosen to live gives her peace.

When we soften our footprint on the earth, our change creates more change. Every earth-conscious choice heals the earth, rather than taking from it. Committing to taking action should never feel like we're giving ourselves a hard time. Instead, it's the beginning of a journey that leads to a safer future. It doesn't have to be loud. It's a very personal commitment and to stay on course, in a society where the loudest message we hear is to consume more, takes a determination and toughness that we're not yet used to living.

Try imperfectly

Celebrate yourself for every choice you make and action you take that goes further towards changing your behaviour. No one is living a perfect green life, but when we act with earth consciousness, we reverse the endless consumption pattern of humans in the world. We begin where our lives touch the planet. Our first step is to lessen that impact.

I'll share with you some of the commitments I have made. These are practices that I try to keep whilst never being mean to myself for those times when I don't. It's not about making a stick to beat ourselves or our less earth-conscious friends with. It's about becoming aware of our red lines and living in ways that don't transgress them. It's about choosing for ourselves how we want to respond to the climate and ecological emergency.

When we do this, we can feel really good about our choices, because if we who consume the most make big changes, it has a significant impact. However, I'm not going to spend a long time listing all the eco-conscious things you can do. There are plenty of books that have already done that, and perhaps you already know what your next steps could be.

Instead, I'll tell you some of the reasons why I've made certain commitments. Take them as suggestions for earth-friendly things you could do. I've found it reassuring to have areas in my life where I have complete control over my ecological footprint. By bringing our attention to these moments where our decisions affect the planet, we begin down the road of changing our relationship to the earth.

Our food

More than 25 per cent of total global emissions are generated from what we eat. Food is also the primary driver of the ecological emergency through destruction of habitats to create monoculture farms. Fertilisers kill the oceans and pesticides are pushing insects and other creatures to extinction. On top of that, one third of all food produce is wasted.

We eat three times a day. Each meal we have can be a moment when our lives protect the earth. Cut down on — and set a deadline for cutting out — meat. Increase the number of days your menu is fully plant-based. Try not to waste anything you buy.

Our clothes

Fashion consumption is set to grow 63 per cent by 2030. Clothes production already accounts for more emissions than aviation and shipping combined. It also has big hidden human and environmental costs, devastating farmers and exploiting low wages and dangerous working conditions in factories.

Reset your relationship with fashion. Take one year off buying any new fashion or textiles. Create space to upcycle, clothes swap, rummage through charity shops and use your own fashion skills to mend or refresh your clothes. If you do buy something, take time to treat yourself and spend extra money so that it's high quality and will last you for years.

Our gadgets

Electronics are replaced way more often than they need to be. Often when we throw them away they go to landfill rather than recycling the precious metals they contain. There's a lengthy history of human-rights abuses both in the mines where precious metals are extracted and the factories where the electronics are assembled.

Keep a list of the things you need. Don't confuse what you actually need with the pressure to buy new gadgets all the time. If you do need a new piece of tech then spend some time researching what is the most durable and easy-to-repair model. I'm going to give a shout-out here to my favourite, the Fairphone.

Our transport

Transport makes up almost one quarter of greenhouse gas emissions, and two thirds of this comes from private vehicles. Car ownership is expected to double by 2040. We need to turn this around.

If you are non-disabled and live in an area that is well served by public transport, please think deeply about whether you need a car. The majority of journeys in the UK are less than two miles. Replace those journeys and go on foot. We can cycle, walk or use public transport. We can join car clubs or create community by sharing rides. If you do need a car then look after it; cars can last for more than 20 years.

Our holidays

Aviation currently generates 2 per cent of global emissions and this amount is growing faster than any other form of transport. Most people don't fly but some people fly a lot. In the UK 70 per cent of all flights are taken by just 15 per cent of the population. People who fly a lot need to fly a lot less.

This doesn't mean never fly (although that may be a red line for you). Just don't fly short-haul — we need to overcome the culture of weekend city breaks. Take a long-haul return flight once every eight years and make it a special trip. Try not to book any new flights. Instead take the train and make the journey part of the adventure. We're all used to video calls with our loved ones now. Keep it up.

Our energy

All energy should be green but as long as it isn't, we can invest in replacing fossil fuels with renewable energy by supporting renewable energy companies. I'm with Ecotricity and I've been a happy customer for years, but this isn't an endorsement of any one company. Research green energy companies and choose the tariff that works best for you.

Our savings

Our banks and pensions are invested in high-carbon infrastructure and industries. It is the job of government and big business to transform the systems on which our society is built, but you can assess what you have control of and, through that, help to shift the wider system. If your bank or pension fund invests in fossil fuels then get in touch with them. Threaten to move your money if they don't make ethical and environmentally sound investments — and make sure to tell them when you follow through on your threat so they know people are serious.

Eco joy

Joy is contagious. It's attractive when we make meaningful commitments and when people can see that we feel good about our impact on the planet. You don't need to be preachy to have conversations with your friends and family and inspire them to change with you. We all know that an individual action won't save the world, but individual actions build a culture where new ways of being are celebrated and, in turn, inspire others to change.

3
What's stopping us?

People have always been good at imagining the end of the world, which is much easier to picture than the strange sidelong paths of change in a world without end.

Rebecca Solnit, *Hope in the Dark*

There's a lot that makes change difficult, not least that we human beings like things to stay the same. The majority of our society has been built on the assumption that we burn fossil fuels to provide energy, and that natural resources are used to create human stuff. It's going to take slow and steady work to dislodge these assumptions that are baked into everything we do. It's going to need courage, determination and optimism to keep on treading into the unknown.

Powerful people have the most to lose

One thing that would make it easier is if the people with the most power were playing their part. Unfortunately, they're not. Instead they're confusing things by heaping blame on us. We're told all the time to change our behaviour, even though just 20 companies are behind a third of all carbon emissions. It's a brilliant sleight of hand. Instead of demanding that these companies change their business model — or go out of business — we agonise over whether we're putting single-use plastic in the right bin.

We look around us and we see a world that is not changing fast enough. We worry that if we have to persuade every single person on our street, or in our city, to change their lives and habits, then we will never get where we need to go. Hope begins to fade as our individual lifestyle changes feel futile. We're told it's our responsibility even though we don't own shares in fossil-fuel resources or make decisions about whether we spend public money on developing low-carbon transport like trains rather than building more roads.

The people with the power to lead us to a different future have been making us feel awful by telling us that we're to blame for the climate and ecological emergency. We're not. When we discover that we can't save the world alone and ask the powerful to lead, they wring their hands and tell us that now is not a good time. Waiting for their leadership has wasted years and even now, when the climate emergency has been widely understood, there is no compelling top-down vision for how we are going to step off the hamster wheel of infinite consumption. We need to come together and make demands of the powerful because left to their own devices, they will lead us to ruin.

Build our courage muscle

Climate change is scary. More and more people are suffering from climate anxiety and this can paralyse us. I want to get better at breathing and then acting even when I feel scared, because action is the best strategy for healing climate anxiety. When we're doing something about climate change, we are connected to the present and we are creating reasons for hope. When we participate in practical actions our minds don't become overwhelmed by a future we don't know yet.

It takes courage to do something about climate change, and my generation, who grew up reading *Vice*, haven't found that courage yet. We prefer to sneer at collective action rather than get involved in it. We'd rather be cynics than optimists.

We don't want to quit our jobs, eat root vegetables, retreat from society or get arrested and so we throw our hands up and do nothing. But the reality of change isn't so black and white. What's actually needed is for us all to think specifically about what we can do, and then find the courage to do it. Not leaping backwards to some pre-industrial age, but slowly walking forwards into a new reality that we will build together.

The only way is through

I guess the crux of it is that we don't want to give up on this reality just yet. There's a lot that we're still happy to enjoy. I don't really have an argument against this. It's more that I don't believe this reality will make me happy for the long term. I can't ignore the news about devastating weather events. I can't forget the science about climate change increasing natural disasters. I feel uneasy when I pretend that the future isn't going to challenge us. Instead I want to prepare.

When we change our habits, our beliefs change too. Instead of having to be a successful individual, I've begun to ask how I can be part of a thriving human story. It will be possible to transition from a climate-changing, extractive economy to one that is circular and prioritises care, but we won't get to this future alone.

The miracle of collective action

Throughout history, human progress has happened when we come together and fight injustice. It's when we overcome exclusive and self-serving elites. The many gather and we fight impossible odds. We win and this slow churn of history takes us away from oppression and towards more freedom for more people. Now there's never been a more important time to be ambitious in our fight for justice. We have all of our futures and all future generations to protect.

In my own life, I've experienced what happens when movements win. I know it's possible for unimaginable futures to become true. I grew up in a school at a time when Section 28 meant I was shamed for trying to talk to my teacher about being queer. I still remember how wrong I felt when I told her I was gay and she went quiet and walked out of the room.

A lot has happened since then. Section 28 is history and there are anti-homophobic bullying policies in schools. Gay marriage has been legalised in many countries around the world. Queer love has become part of the cultural mainstream and we are fighting to protect trans children.

Now, I'm a non-binary person married to a woman in an area of London that has a queer community and our own 'Forest Gayte Pride'. I'm able to have sensitive conversations with my parents, the people who I thought my sexuality and gender identity would disappoint the most. One day my wife and I will adopt a child or children. It's unlikely we'll be discriminated against but if we suspect that we are, we'll take the adoption services to court and win.

The world has been changed by billions of people opening their minds to realities beyond what they were told was 'normal'. I get a lot of hope from charting this progress. It's not enough and there are still enormous mountains to climb, especially where queer identities intersect with other marginalised identities, but there is movement and most of us, in some small way, have been affected by and influential in that movement. We made this 'normal' happen. We made it happen and we can stop it from happening. We are the common denominator in what stops and starts change.

Start here: 5 ways to soften your footprint on the earth

The most important action you can take is to begin, and to not give up on that beginning.

Choose a commitment from the list of five below. Set a reminder in your diary or online calendar for three months' time. Check in then with how you are doing. Celebrate and choose another two commitments. Or, if you have let your commitments drop, then use this 90-day reminder to reset your intention to heal your relationship with the earth.

1. **Have one day a week when your whole menu is plant-based (vegan).** If that's too big a step then take two days a week to be fully vegetarian.

2. **Replace short journeys with walking, cycling or public transport.** Whilst you're out, listen for birdsong and identify the trees.

3. **Research the climate and ecological emergency.** Tell someone what you've found out and also what you are doing about it in at least one conversation each week.

4. **Take one year off any of the following** (start with a year; hopefully this will be the beginning of the end for these high-carbon practices): buying new clothes; taking short-haul flights; holidaying abroad; eating meat (especially beef); buying new tech.

5. **Get a hold of your finances.** Make sure that your money is not funding the climate and ecological emergency. Choose a green energy tariff. If your bank or pension fund invests in fossil fuels, change your investments.

Tear this page out and stick it to your fridge.

What we do is more important than what we say or what we say we believe.

—

bell hooks

What I want does exist if I dare to find it.

—

Jeanette Winterson, *Why Be Happy When You Could Be Normal*

COMMUNITY

4
Together
we stand

We've seen that the planet and all who live on it are approaching an era of unprecedented crisis. In response to this, individually and as a society, we are looking for ways to heal rather than extract. But even when our planet regenerates, the cost of climate change means we will experience more and fiercer natural disasters. The impact of these disasters will create new tensions between us.

One of our biggest fears is about our safety and the safety of those we love. As individualism has become aspirational, we've begun to doubt whether we can be happy without being selfish. Too often, seizing what we want is prioritised above building collective wellbeing and so we begin to worry that our safety depends on our selfishness.

But this version of the world isn't our only reality. True security will come when we can trust that there is food, shelter, connection and beauty now and way into the future. It's a world where we won't need to fear that people will hoard things or exclude us from what they have. The most practical thing to do when things get scarce is to build interdependent and resilient communities that leave no one behind, because without these, all we will do is fight.

In a world that is becoming less hospitable, the only way we'll trust that we are secure is by creating strong communities that provide for each other. We won't have good lives if we're scared of each other and trying to get through crises alone. We'll feel safe when our communities are resilient and prioritising care.

However large or small our friendship circle, family, local community or work network might be, it's time to think with intention about who we spend time with and whether that time contributes to community resilience.

We're not used to thinking intentionally about our relationships. Instead, we accumulate friends and family as we move from childhood through education and into our adult life. But to live well through challenging contexts, we need to be more attentive to the connections we are building. Community is a promise that we will not abandon each other. Are there people in your life who you have made this promise to?

Beyond immediate family

Most of us don't have a big community. There's perhaps our romantic partner, immediate family and a couple of close friends. We prioritise a handful of conventional relationships: the Hollywood romance that develops into a family with 2.4 children (this story has been so amplified that it can seem like the only serious relationships worth investing in). This has meant that other relationship narratives, which expand outwards into the community, have not been told.

Many of my queer friends didn't have a choice about expanding their community. Rejected by their immediate family, they had to develop trusted and supportive relationships with other people. These people became their 'chosen family'. I have friends who are as important to me as my blood relatives. We will be there for each other, whatever the future brings. My chosen family grows and grows, stretching beyond the people I grew up with to include those I want to care for me and give love to.

We need to become experts at creating loving relationships both within and beyond our immediate family. These relationships will help us cope in unknown ways through the uncharted territory of our collective future. Practical love is the essential ingredient for thriving through the challenges that are coming and those that are already here.

Towards greater resilience

In practice, when disaster hits, the best of our humanity jumps to the rescue. Whether it's the community organising that brought food and water to the most vulnerable following Hurricane Sandy or the thousands of self-organised mutual aid groups that grew up and looked after people throughout the 2020/21 Covid-19 pandemic, we build vibrant and resilient communities when we are on the knife-edge of disaster. Our challenge is to build this resilience into our everyday lives alongside one another, rather than crossing our fingers that it will emerge when disaster strikes.

Global events remind us of how vulnerable we are and how much we rely on often too thin reserves of resilience. The isolated and independent self as the aspirational social unit does not serve us when we need to cope collectively with unprecedented change. When we challenge 'the individual' by building community there are so many social goods, not least a path away from an epidemic of loneliness that is attacking us.

Community offers support when times are hard and celebrates when times are good. This solidarity is something I long for from those around me and feel enriched by when I receive. Other people's support and good opinion causes my whole self to glow.

Get specific about the communities that you belong to and what your involvement brings. Watch out for the dynamics at play in your family, your work, local community, sports community, political groups, online networks and more. Begin to think about how your participation could make the group dynamics healthier and more resilient.

Creating communities that give us what we need

Some of the most nourishing relationships that exist in my life have been created because I made a decision to set aside time for them. Instead of relying on the pre-existing relationships of family, work and hobbies, I created or participated in spaces where the primary purpose was to care for each other and elevate mutual support. If the only relationships in your life are those connected to family and work, then I encourage you to look for supportive spaces that prioritise community and care. Two examples that I participate in are book club and sharing circles.

There are plenty of ways to begin a book club and hundreds that already exist if you seek them out online. The most important step I took when creating one was to decide what it was I wanted to learn about and then to find the people who wanted to learn about that thing with me.

It began because a friend and I decided we needed a better understanding of social theory. We Googled for a reading list, chose one, posted on social media that we were starting a book club and anyone was welcome, and then created a WhatsApp group for the people who were interested. Then we began.

Once we had gone through the pretty dry reading list of social theorists that we'd found online, we made our own list of books by women of colour. Audre Lorde, bell hooks and Reni Eddo-Lodge became part of our learning landscape. Our worlds were enriched as we delighted in the education that we had chosen together to begin. If you're still quite new to understanding the impacts of climate, then why not start a book club with a reading list that includes books about how we can respond to the climate and ecological emergency?

Sharing circles are where I learn that I can cope with the anxiety of living in a world full of crisis. Inspired by 12-step groups and other forms of group therapy, they are communities for collective healing and nothing else. Governed by mutually agreed rules (a three-minute limit for sharing, that what is said in the circle stays in the circle and that no unsolicited advice is given once the circle is closed), I sit with people I have come to know for one hour a week and we listen to each other speak.

We share our thoughts on a reading, a topic, or we just say whatever it is we need to say in that moment, on that day. We hear other people's pain and feel able to share the things that we're scared we shouldn't say. All of our honesty creates a space that feels radical because of the rawness of the personal truths that are spoken. We listen to each other and when we leave the circle we feel connected to the tenderest parts of our and their humanity.

If you don't have anything like a book club or a sharing circle in your life and the networks that you are part of are more functional than healing, then I encourage you to make space for one of these. Create one or find one that's already established and see if it doesn't offer rest to your soul.

5
**My
neighbourhood**

No one knows everything but together we know a whole lot.

Simon Sinek

If we try to tackle the climate and ecological emergency alone and all at once, we're likely to get burnt out. As individuals we can't change the whole world, but we can come together to create neighbourhoods where we make it easier for people to live in earth-conscious ways.

Our challenge is to redesign human communities so that we are in sync with the world around us and to have a strong vision of how good and nourishing these neighbourhoods could be. Just imagine if recycling were as easy as a weekly collection — that took plastics, glass, metal, paper, fabrics, wood and all your garden and food waste — from outside your front door. If your local walks were to wildflower meadows through tree-lined streets with biodiversity-enriched borders. If public transport were publicly owned and cheap, and if we were all financially rewarded for ditching our car and using our feet instead.

Already there are people in your local area who are writing to the council about initiatives such as these. They might need a bit more people power to win. They might be waiting for someone like you to help them out. If you do get involved in community actions, I hope you'll find (like I did) that winning campaigns is just a small part of the story. Even better than the victories are the relationships you form.

When we engage directly with people one-on-one and have conversations, we create space to discover that we share common goals. As a healing strategy, this gives us such deep nourishment, to realise that we can join forces with people who long for the same things that we are longing for.

Community exists just outside your front door. Once something is happening locally, many more people will want to get involved. It's going to take all of us to create resilient communities and, as with most things, the most important step is the first one we take.

Mobilise around a cause

About ten years ago I started community organising in Newham. It's one of the most deprived and diverse boroughs in the United Kingdom. My reason for getting involved was that it's home to London City Airport which had been trying to expand. I wanted to mobilise the local community against its expansion.

I have one friend who cares as much about stopping airport expansion as me. Her name is Alice and over the years she's taught me a lot about consistency. When she makes promises, she keeps them — which means she's careful about the promises she makes. Through her example the penny finally dropped. Instead of promising the world and under-delivering, I'm now careful to offer what I know I can give.

Way back in 2009, I persuaded Alice to come and knock on doors with me. We prepared a small script about the impacts of the airport and we had objection letters that we asked residents to sign. We also had a spreadsheet for people to add their name to if they wanted to get more involved with our campaign.

After a weekend of door-knocking we had over a hundred objection letters. Two households had invited us in for food and refreshment. We'd also realised that the airport's expansion was not a priority for this community. They wanted public services, a better library, a park where their children could play, more jobs and training for their community.

A local schoolteacher put us in touch with Amina, an ex-student of hers who she thought would want to get involved. We met Julie, a single mum who lived opposite the perimeter fence of the airport, and who became one of our most furious (and brilliant) volunteers. When a local community centre heard about what we were doing and offered us space to anchor our community organising, we couldn't believe our luck.

From two people finding the courage and energy to go and knock on doors, a local community initiative had begun. We called it 'The Momentum Project'. Every Wednesday night people from the community and their kids met in the centre. Shouting above the noise of the kids, we tried to make plans for involving more local people in our campaigns.

Move where the energy is

It was Amina who got the kids singing. She's a professional singer, so she volunteered to keep the kids busy by starting a choir. In one of the centre's rooms the Royal Docks Singstars was born. With Amina's direction, the children found their voices and used them to sing in the community choir every week. They learnt about how to sing in harmony, how to let others lead, and how to come together for a crescendo.

Amina is an extraordinary teacher and organiser. She wrote a song with the kids called 'Always Believe' — and it was so beautiful to watch them learn and sing words about their own resilience and potential. Under her guidance the Royal Docks Singstars became a choir that headlined TEDxNewham, competed in talent shows at the Newham Mayor's Show and performed on stage at the Royal Festival Hall.

The parents didn't have to worry about childcare and, whilst the kids sang, they organised campaigns and shared food with each other. We made plans, built a community garden and gathered thousands of objection letters against the airport. The front door of people's houses had been a barrier but soon we made it a threshold — somewhere to have conversations and invite more community action.

In the streets surrounding London City Airport we were building the sort of community power that I'd always longed to be part of. The cause that had got me involved in this neighbourhood was climate change, specifically campaigning against the expansion of London City Airport, but the real healing power of community organising meant that we all felt less alone.

More and more I recognised people from the community projects that were emerging. It felt like The Momentum Project had opened a floodgate and now other initiatives were popping up. People were discovering that by asking for something, they stood a chance of getting it. When I smiled at people, I began to trust that despite our different backgrounds we had a shared vision and principles that connected us.

This feeling of belonging to a mixed group of people and a local area was so good that it wasn't long before I moved across London — from Camden to Newham — so that I could participate more fully in the community that we were creating.

The fate of London City Airport remains unresolved. Its expansion plans have been cancelled, green-lit and paused indefinitely since we knocked on people's doors back in 2009. It's a long road for an airport that feels increasingly out of place and out of date. And whilst London City Airport struggles against the limitations of its inner-city location, the tools and support we found whilst building our campaign endure, enriching my understanding of community and resilience.

With action, dreams come true

In my years of activism, it's moments like these that I've found most rewarding; when I'm part of a group — leaving no-one behind — that works towards significant change. It never happens overnight and it takes some organising but with consistent community action, we can change our local area.

An easy place to start might be to approach your local council. Ask them what they're doing about the climate and ecological emergency. It should be a priority, so use your community voice to get them on a more environmental track. For the most part, our local governments are responsive to their constituents (i.e. you!). It doesn't take a lot to let them know what you want to see in your local area and then to put a little pressure on them to achieve those goals.

Friends of the Earth created a guide of 33 actions that every council could take to get them on track to a zero-carbon future.[3] We can use this to inspire our own dreams about what our local area would look like, if our councils were working for the planet and our futures. When we begin to imagine a better future locally, we can find the courage to demand that it happens.

Your area can be a place that is setting the agenda for community resilience and environmental neighbourhoods. From electric buses to space for cycling and pedestrians, from community-owned, renewable energy projects to divesting from fossil fuels, from bringing nature into our public spaces to requiring that buildings do not leak energy, we can demand our dream neighbourhood.

And if the council drags its feet, then by coming together, we can take action that guides our representatives towards healthier policy decisions.

Gather with community

There are people in your area who are already organising, just as there are people hungry for the sort of purpose and connection that community organising provides. If you're timid to start something, have a look at what's already out there. There will be local community Facebook groups, a monthly litter pick and other active groups that are organising around the environment. Don't reinvent the wheel; instead take time to find out what's already happening that you can contribute to.

Organise walks, harvest food, cook meals and use collective political power to heal our local environment. Together our voices can demand change from local and

---

3   policy.friendsoftheearth.uk/insight/33-actions-local-authorities-can-take-climate-change

national government (as well as all the businesses who rely on our consumer power). By getting together with other people, we begin to heal the isolation that has become an ache at the heart of our society. We also stand a much better chance of making our local area a better place to live.

Know what you're trying to change

There is power in achieving things together. This power can never be reached by doing something alone. It's a power that we need to kindle wherever we find it and one way to do that is by fighting campaigns that we can win. Set a timeframe and celebrate any small victories along the way. Make rituals of those celebrations. Reflect on why you won and share your best practices with as wide an audience as possible so that you inspire more organisers.

Keep a sustainable pace and adopt practices that grow your community's resilience. This will mean that even when it seems like nothing is changing, you'll be able to hold on tight to each other and stay the course until the weight of your organising crashes through and miracles happen.

Prioritise food, ritual and friendship

The fine balance of organising is to make the group and its dynamic as central to its purpose as the activities that the group does together. Yes, we want to be part of a community that is collectively making the world better — through outreach, learning, actions and campaigns — but we also want to be part of a community so that we can care and feel cared for, heal and be healed.

Begin your meetings by setting an intention for that meeting. Invite different people in the group to choose and bring a reading, poem, prayer or song to set the tone. Start each meeting with such an offering. Intimacy is what we risk so that we can build trust. Invite people to check in and share how things are going for them that day. Build rituals that give a sense of purpose and belonging to your meetings. Remember that at any point in a meeting you can pause to take a shared breath, to stretch and move from the restless pace of your mind back into the peace of your body.

Never underestimate the power of cooking and eating together. Include being with each other in your planning time. Community organising isn't just about winning campaigns but building a place that feels as good as home. Use ritual to honour and make tangible our connections to one another. Honour the relationships that we are creating, because our current culture doesn't honour these relationships enough. This is a big deal and it does take commitment and work, so weave love and gratitude for each other into the fabric of your work.

If you need more local support, go out and get it

If there's something that you're longing to see in your neighbourhood, tell people about it. Some of these things can be won by lobbying the local council, but others you can create for yourself with a small group of people. In my area we have a monthly litter pick, a community garden, a Jumble Trail and a local Pride march that takes place once a year. All these initiatives now enjoy the support of the local council but they began with ordinary people giving their time to make a good idea happen.

This community activity has made my neighbourhood somewhere dynamic and friendly, where I know that if I need help I can reach out to people who live nearby. Over the 2020/21 pandemic we put leaflets through every door in our street and became part of the mutual aid group that shopped and cooked for our most vulnerable neighbours. Living in an area where your feeling of safety comes from knowing that people will look out for you is so healing.

If you have a petition and you need to get a certain number of signatures on it to make the local council take notice, consider gathering a group and going in pairs door to door. Fear of knocking on a stranger's door is an internal barrier that we can overcome. It's only recently that we've come to consider people who live on our streets as strangers; they used to be our neighbours.

We need to bring the neighbourhood back and if you have a petition that could make your local area a better place, then you're doing everyone a favour by finding the courage to knock on your neighbours' doors.

Community meetings

It's a big deal to begin to reimagine our communities, to go out and be active participants in them. None of this happens in a day and if it's to happen at all then we'll need to work together. If we're to bring people together, support one another and pool resources, then we need to lay our devils aside and start working at being our kindest, most collaborative selves. There's preparation we can do to make it easier to find and rely on our better selves. The design of our meetings creates the culture of our groups.

Over the years I've been part of a lot of groups that have had terrible meeting practices. This has meant that meetings felt like a drain on energy rather than an inspiring and invigorating event. But if we start the meeting by asking everyone to check in and share how they're doing that day, then we get to hear something honest from everyone before we even begin. That intimacy can create something gentle at the heart of the group.

We can encourage people to lead and to step into their power, whilst remaining aware of how quickly ego and self-righteous certainty can shrivel a group dynamic. We can allow the purpose (rather than the individual) to take centre stage. There is nothing attractive about a group dynamic that allows one person to take up all the space. We need to find ways to keep deflating that ego.

MY NEIGHBOURHOOD

We learn how to facilitate so that we can all hold meeting spaces without needing to be the centre of them. We practise consensus decision-making so that everyone is part of the decisions that are taken and we are all committed to those decisions.

If you have no experience of facilitating a meeting then take some time to look at trainings online. Seeds for Change [4] are a wonderful resource for learning how to be a great facilitator. Invite everyone to contribute to the ground rules and establish them together — such as a timed limit for people to speak, a clearly time-framed agenda that everyone agrees to stick to, time set aside for any other business and a system where people who want to speak put their hands up and get chosen in order.

When new people show up, tell them that they are welcome and find out what they have come to do. Let them do that thing. Keep reiterating the ground rules so that everyone gets a chance to speak and many chances to listen. Allow the direction of the group to be guided by your shared

---

4   www.seedsforchange.org.uk/resources

purpose rather than by some fixed notion of what you should be doing. Keep asking the group how to make our working together a healing practice.

Protect your boundaries

We all suffer from negative voices invading our brains, telling us that we're imposters, that we don't belong and that there is no way we can change the world. We might feel like nothing we're doing is good enough, or else we feel like we're doing everything and no one is appreciating us. Our inadequacy or our frustration becomes the loudest voice in our head.

We can't stand these feelings and so we give up and walk away or turn on each other, gossip and talk negatively. We start to judge those who aren't moving at our pace. At these moments (and they will come), we need to notice that we're acting on behalf of these mean and judgemental voices in our heads. When it gets to this stage we need to stop.

We need instead to be so gentle with all the feelings that working alongside other people provokes, both in us and in them. We're going to need to become experts at holding space for each other and working together. This emotional labour is what will allow us to create spaces where we can come together and heal. Our future resilience will be built in these spaces. It's not just one person's job to keep the group dynamic healthy and moving forward. We all need to show up, knowing that we are secure in our own boundaries.

Boundaries allow us to remain intact. By learning how to say no, we can really mean it and commit when we say yes. We need to say no so that when we do say yes, we're saying it with all our strength and passion. We must watch out for when we are acting like radiators and when we are acting like drains. By staying within our boundaries we can do what we want rather than what we think people want of us. We keep enough warmth for ourselves and discover that we can ask for help without becoming dependent on someone else's heat.

We practise these healing strategies to help us be, and work, together. By looking after ourselves we show others that it's right for them to look after themselves too. We create community spaces that feel great to be part of and together we begin to make our local areas a better place to live. Then, when the resilient communities that we are trying to create begin to buddy up, we'll be halfway there.

6
What does winning feel like?

Our struggles are particular, but we are not alone.

Audre Lorde, *Sister Outsider*

There's no gold medal in community organising. Instead, as our local area becomes a friendlier and greener place to be, we all win. We get practical experience of feeling bound to our neighbours, knowing that our wellbeing is bound up with theirs. It's not the heady success of throwing everything at a one-time victory, instead it is a slow journey made with other people to enrich the community.

This is deeply counter-cultural work. We let go of ego and the cult of the individual, and turn towards service, collective action and shared victories. There are moments of celebration along the way but it's not all easy or light. We build a toughness that comes because we are also sharing (and learning how to cope with) sorrow, frustration and grief. Our victories are not one moment or one fight won, but a turning away from individualism and towards the woven threads of resilient community.

Better teachers

> Disabled people are experts in finding new ways
> to do things when the old ways don't work. We are
> a vast think tank right in plain sight. A bottomless
> well of ingenuity and creativity.

Riva Lehrer

We look to people who survive impossible conditions to show us that we can make things happen that we were told were impossible. By centring the experience and wisdom of disabled people, BIPOC (Black, Indigenous, people of colour) people, survivors of racism, xenophobia, gender discrimination, homophobia and poverty, we learn how to live beyond the systems that we have right now.

When we learn strategies of self-care and community support it's important to remember that the marginalised communities who first developed these healing strategies did so as a matter of survival. Our lives and happiness were threatened by a status quo that excluded us from the dominant model of 'normal'. We weren't celebrated by popular culture and never saw people like us holding positions of power.

People who have been rejected by the status quo find so many creative ways to heal the trauma of not belonging. We create counter-cultures with ambitions outside society's model of success. Instead of prioritising individualistic success, these alternative cultures value and develop rich networks of support, community, friendship and connection.

We have a lot to learn from people who, in a world of patriarchy, capitalism and white supremacy, were never going to be 'winners'. Since they were never going to win, they created a different game of life with different rules. Rules like refusing perfectionism, building community beyond the immediate family and learning how to rest (so they could fight for their lives the next day). Black feminists, disabled people and trans people are pathfinders to new worlds because when this world, that dominates the earth to survive, rejected them, they rejected the practice of domination.

Freedom to choose

We'll know successful community by how it feels. There's no coercion, instead people are drawn in because we're somewhere good to belong. Instead of asking what we can get out of it or feeling resentful that we've overpromised, we come because we have skills that we know are useful.

Together we map our skills. We offer what we have. We do what we can, not what we think we should. We recognise needs in the community that we can fill. The list is endless for what these might be: the ability to comfort, hold someone's hand, cook or serve food; provide a space where people can meet, or the ability to translate the community newsletter or Facebook posts into languages that reach everyone within the neighbourhood.

There is no moment of victory. Using capitalism's measuring scales, we find that we won't ever win, so instead we build a different model of success. We ask ourselves whether we're being enriched. We ask whether there is more trust in our area. Are we facing in the direction of a kinder, more resilient world? We listen and we follow our hearts. We build community where we find it and where we've been missing it for years.

How a small group can make a place better

If you've contacted the local council but they just aren't budging, then here are five steps to guide you in creating an undeniable campaign.

1. **Map what already exists.** Gather all the data for community organisations active in your area, from political parties to grassroots groups to parent groups and faith organisations. Use Google and social media to get the details of everyone who is organising locally.

2. **Identify a campaign with broad-based appeal that you can win.** Whether you are supporting a campaign that already exists or proposing a new campaign for or against something in your neighbourhood, make sure you're choosing something that common sense supports. Who is the decision-maker (i.e. the target of your campaign), and what clearly and specifically are you asking them to do?

3. **Reach out to the active community organisers and organisations** that you mapped out in step 1. Write a short invitation asking that they support your campaign and asking for access to their membership so you can speak or write directly to their supporters/audience. Follow up your written invitation with a phone call or a request to meet face to face.

4. **Gather community support** through petitions, letter-writing campaigns and eye-catching protest actions. These are the tools we can use to win campaigns. Every time you use one of these tools, gather your

community, share what you are doing on social media and send pictures and captions to your local media.

5. **Figure out what a sustainable momentum is for your community and maintain it.** Try not to lose focus and remember to celebrate — within your house, your community and across social media — every moment along your campaign's journey. Apply consistent pressure on the decision-makers. By reminding your decision-makers that they are accountable to the community, you have already won.

When I'm happy it is good for the world: we show and encourage that there is another way that isn't full of stress, self-doubt, pain, victimization and suffering. There is a path where *all* is learning, playing, practicing, easy and light.

—

adrienne maree brown, *Pleasure Activism*

EARTH

7
The hollow tree

In the middle of Hampstead Heath there is a hollow tree. It wasn't until 2020 — the year when we all got better acquainted with our cities' green spaces — that I was shown this tree. My friend Shelley took me there. She's not just my friend. She's also my spiritual guide. I call her Yoda and she laughs and then sends me a stream of *Star Wars* memes. She knows how much I love trees and so she suggested we go and find the hollow tree on Hampstead Heath, London's biggest and wildest park.

It was late autumn and the trees were shedding their canopies. Red and brown leaves were being trodden into thick brown mud. Earthworms were weaving a way through the mulch and in the dank forest floor thousands of fungi flowered. Our boots were caked in mud and with each step we pulled ourselves free, remembering to look up as we stumbled.

We made slow progress. I like to walk fast but with Shelley that isn't an option. Every step she takes places her in a new world of wonder and she takes her time, appreciating what she can see from the new perspective she's placed herself in. When I'm at her side, I can't rush, and gradually what was a frustratingly slow pace becomes a meditative experience. I let myself be in nature — not passing through, or on my way — but instead just to be.

It was one of those clear autumn days when the sun is low and orange and the sky particularly blue. The near naked branches of the trees let the light in to the forest floor. Branches that had chosen their route to more sunshine were exposed, the crevices in the bark casting shadows and the moss on the south side of the tree trunks sinking the sun's light.

When we reached the hollow tree, we approached as though it were an altar. It stood in the middle of a gently trodden path but for the time we spent there, no one passed. From each angle the tree looked completely different. We circled it, following its curve around; smooth, strong bark gave way to gnarled protrusions that looked like the distorted features of a gargoyle. We came closer and held our arms around the tree, hugging it. The circumference of this oak was so big that even with both our arms outstretched we couldn't fit around it.

Shelley told me to climb inside, laughing at a rumour she'd heard that 15 drunk people had once managed to get stuck in there. I took hold of the outer bark and wrapped my fingers around the smooth varnish of its inside surface. I hoisted myself up and into the tree. The wood inside was sculptural, intricately shaped and shining as though it had been polished. Discovering different textures beneath my fingertips I felt a satisfaction that I could rest here for years. Outside Shelley kept her hands on the trunk and together we said, 'Thank you, hollow tree.'

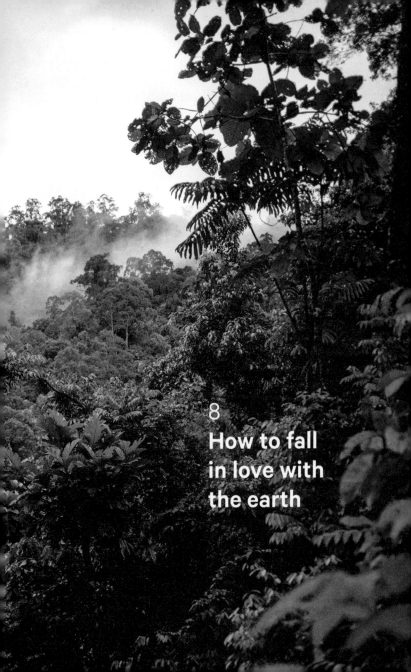

8
**How to fall
in love with
the earth**

The universe is God's self-portrait.

Octavia E. Butler, 'Earthseed' verse from
Parable of the Sower

When we're ready to learn, nature will teach us everything we need to know about how to relate to each other, the earth and ourselves. When we're ready, the earth will show us how to heal.

Dying nature creates new ecosystems. Dead trees provide habitat, cycle nutrients, regenerate plants, capture carbon and keep soil wet. Nature is abundant and the different elements within it create a dance of balance and reciprocity. When nature is in charge, everything is what it is and exactly what it should be.

However hard we try to think our way out of it, we are natural creatures too. We rebel against this, burdened as we are with fretful brains. Collectively we have exerted our power to dominate everything, including our earth.

There is much for us to relearn and remember from nature. Even in these times, the earth is so rich. If we were to stop waste, celebrate generosity and condemn greed, we can imagine a world of plenty. It's not so far away. The biggest step to getting there will be when we stop trying to bend nature to our fears of scarcity and instead open ourselves up to her patterns of abundance.

Take the long view

We're stuck in habits that have started to feel like dead-ends. Nature blows a way through and leads us to age-old healing practices like the acceptance of change, curiosity, interdependence, resilience and patience. We can all be more like the bulb in winter, accepting and respecting the seasons and trusting that new and beautiful life will come.

We can look to the earth and to the people who have not severed their intelligence from the earth's wisdom. Indigenous people have been stewards of the planet for thousands of years. According to a *National Geographic* article, they make up less than 5 per cent of the global population and yet the land they dwell on supports more than 80 per cent of global biodiversity. Where Indigenous people have been living, nature has continued to thrive. We should be listening to their philosophies and amplifying them throughout all our cultures, whether in urban or rural settings. We need to learn from Indigenous people to stop assaulting biodiversity and to re-establish a reciprocal relationship with our planet.

One of the most widely repeated Native American philosophies is the seventh-generation principle. It's based on the Haudenosaunee (Iroquois) Great Law of Peace (Gayanashagowa). The principle states that we should make decisions about how we live today based on how our decisions will impact the next seven generations to come. If we can make practical this principle, we will be good caretakers of the earth, not simply for ourselves, but for those who will inherit the earth and the results of our decisions.

Seven generations is around 140 years away. Between now and then there will be countless decisions made by countless people all trying to secure a life worth living.

The purpose of all these lives will change as new pressures take hold and old pressures are released. It's going to take some careful retuning to orient our lives to care for such future descendants and to learn from people whose ways are channels of earth consciousness.

Mushroom magic

Long before humans were even a twinkle in evolution's eye, giant mushrooms up to 8m high towered over the earth. Mushrooms evolved about 1.3 billion years ago, more than 500 million years before trees and other plants. They are ancient and they are everywhere, decomposing organic matter and transforming it into stuff that can be used by other species.

The mushrooms that we eat are just a small visible part of the fungi organism. The other part, largely invisible to us, is mycelium: a network of fine white filaments that exist like threads in the earth beneath everything. Whenever an organism dies, it is swallowed up and broken down by these threads. That's every leaf, every bug and every fallen tree; everything that decomposes into the nutrients soil needs to be nourished.

The mycelium reproduces on its own, creating spores and, as it grows, it meets another mycelia network to connect with. What happens when these networks connect is magical, intelligent and — to humankind — pretty inexplicable. The mycelia share information about the environment they've grown in with each other. Through this sharing of information the trees and plants that have taken root in the mycelium talk to each other, sending signals to help each other grow, to tell each other where there is disease and to encourage each other to thrive.

These mycelium networks have been connecting all living beings at root for hundreds of millions of years.

I geek out about this because when I walk in nature and feel myself drawn towards a tree, I love imagining its roots plugged into a mycelium network in the soil below. Do the roots transmit my presence to the underground mycelia where all living plants take root? I nerd out about nature's intelligence as one of many ways to respect the richness of the earth I'm treading on. I want to know more so that my appreciation of its magic can grow.

We're all part of this extraordinary intelligence that is perpetually flourishing. When I feel despair about how our lives will turn out and what the legacy of our species will be, I am reassured by remembering my place in nature. If you study any species — fungi, bee, butterfly or seaweed — you'll discover a hundred intricate lessons about how to belong to this planet. We are nature too, and our dissatisfaction with the climate and ecological emergency our species has caused opens up a path where we can better support nature's healing process.

Let nature be

Leaving nature alone is one way we're helping her heal. Rewilding is now understood to be essential to the earth's regeneration. It is built on the hypothesis that wild nature, free from human interference, is more resilient, resourceful and creative than our small imaginations can fathom.

The hypothesis is being proven from National Parks to the lawns in our back gardens. One of the first and best-known examples is the reintroduction of wolves to Yellowstone National Park in Wyoming in 1995. The park was overrun with elk, who with few natural predators had eaten their way through much of the park's vegetation. When the wolves came, they ate some of the elk, allowing the trees to regrow. This created a chain of events that led to more abundance and variety of life in the park.

On a smaller scale, the lawns that we have meticulously kept in our gardens are biodiversity deserts, but when we leave them alone — mowing less frequently and at a higher level (an extra 10cm is enough) — they become wildflower meadows that nurture insects and pollinators with extraordinary speed.

Rewilding isn't about removing humans from the scene. Instead, it's about changing the relationship to create active partnerships with nature where we intervene only to enable maximum ecosystem richness. We can give a helping hand by creating the right conditions — removing dykes and dams to free rivers, reducing active management of wildlife populations, allowing natural forest regeneration, and reintroducing species that have disappeared as a result of human actions. Then we step back and let nature manage itself, because when it comes to survival and self-governance none of us knows better than nature.

Isabella Tree is a pioneer rewilder. She allowed her farm in rural Sussex to return to nature and in doing so became an advocate for the flourishing of nature and the near-to-lost species she saw. She wrote a book, *Wilding*, about her farm and in it we read the perspective of a woman whose journey into nature opened up the peace and humility of recognising her place in it.

She writes:

> *The sound of a single butterfly is imperceptible, but tens of thousands have a breath of their own, like the backdraft of a waterfall or an accumulating weather front. It feels as though the oscillating*

susurration of their wingbeats, pounding away on
their supernatural wavelength, might dissolve the
world into atoms.

I long for the abundance of nature that Isabella Tree describes. When I'm in natural environments, I want my senses to be wide awake to what surrounds them. To do this, I need to develop healing practices so that I can quiet my mind and open myself up to the power that runs through all nature.

9
**Quiet the mind
and notice
miracles**

> **To forget how to dig the earth and to tend the soil is to forget ourselves.**
>
> —
>
> Mahatma Gandhi

As we approach the end of the book, I want to share some practices — daily things that I do which keep me alive to nature. These are healing strategies I engage with so that I can connect more easily to the earth. They're tools I have picked up to still the noise in my head, and help me keep alert, aware and awake to all the magic of the natural world. It's not a comprehensive list, so take what works for you and keep trying out new practices to add to your own toolbox of healing strategies.

Be grateful

When I'm regularly writing a ten-point gratitude list, I look out for and notice moments during the day to be grateful for. During the time that I am physically writing it — for a few minutes each morning or night — I appreciate the simplest pleasures and privileges I have. I celebrate good things that have happened that day. I notice the wonder that can come at any moment and because I've created a practice of noticing it, I'm more likely to walk towards it and celebrate when it comes.

A gratitude list is not complicated. It's as simple as what you ate or what you saw on a walk. It can be the fact that your house is heated, you got a good night's sleep or appreciating the flowers you picked for yourself. Writing it might encourage you to give someone a call — to have a conversation and say something that later you can be grateful you said.

A practice begins with the commitment to try something once. Make tonight the night when you try writing a gratitude list.

Discover through writing

I write to myself all the time. In her book *The Artist's Way*, Julia Cameron suggests writing three pages every morning to get the noise out of your head. Through a daily practice of writing how you feel, you're likely to recognise patterns and give yourself space to commit to plans, hopes and prayers. It's a powerful tool that forces you to slow down and work out how you are.

I feel better the more time I give myself to gently process emotions. With less noise in my head I can be more present in the world around me. Having said that, I rarely write three pages in the morning. My patterns with writing change all the time. Sometimes I'm in a really good place — sitting still and writing about my day every day, celebrating my achievements and noticing behaviours that I want to move beyond.

Other times it's infrequent — writing down quotes that speak to me or creating small rituals around a new moon, new year or any moment that I can fill up with gravitas. At these significant moments, I write about what I would like to leave behind and what I would like to take with me and grow.

Sit and breathe

You should sit in meditation for 20 minutes every day, unless you're too busy; then you should sit for an hour.

Zen Proverb

I hate meditating. I still do it every day. When I began to meditate I would set my alarm for two minutes, sit still and breathe. Over the years I've added minutes until now I meditate for 20 minutes each morning.

The moment I wake up — before I pick up my phone, go to the loo, have a glass of water, anything — I put my back against the bedhead, cross my legs and breathe. When my head is busy with thoughts I try to let go of them.

I relax the muscles around my face — from the top of my skull, working my way down. I scan down my body and tell each section, organ and atom to relax. First the skin that is stretched around my skull, the tension in my temples, all the muscles around my nose, cheeks, eye sockets, tongue, throat and shoulders. I run through each bit of my body and very specifically tell it to drop, to let go and know peace.

Next, I imagine a golden thread emanating from the crown of my head that pulls my spine straight. I know that I can relax because this golden thread is holding me up. I breathe. And then if thoughts flood in, I tell myself my mind is a huge blue sky. I imagine the sky in the back of my head, stretching out behind and beyond me. I tell myself that as thoughts come into my mind — this blue skyscape — they are clouds that are just passing through. I let the thoughts pass through.

I hope I'll grow this practice because I know it gives me space around my thinking to act rather than to react. I notice what my impulses are and what might be prodding at them. I pause before choosing what I want to do. I don't know how it would affect my anxiety if I were to stop meditating and I don't want to find out. Meditation is a moment of peace that — through the commitment of my daily routine — I have got in the habit of finding. It's the soft strength on which the rest of my day is built.

There's no wrong or right way to meditate, though there's plenty of guidance out there to help you begin. I hope you find your space to sit still and breathe.

Turn off your phone

> Beware of the stories you read or tell; subtly, at night, beneath the waters of consciousness, they are altering your world.'
>
> Ben Okri

If you find yourself scrolling through social media or updating news sites endlessly, then it might be time to have a device detox. I don't manage it very often, but it remains true that the best weekends I have are those when I leave my phone in a drawer. I have so many rules around using my phone these days because if I don't, then it won't be long until it is permanently in my hand and distracting me from the life that's happening in front of me. To guard against that I have times each day when I'm on my phone, and the rest of the time I try to leave it alone.

As far as I can work out, there are a couple of big positives about the immediacy of phones and other devices. They can turn anywhere into a library where we get to choose our subject and who is teaching us. They also gather our community all day and all night right there at our fingertips.

Of course, tools that make education and connection effortless are great, but I'm suspicious about whether these devices actually offer that. Learning and connecting take time and attention. We can't do either well when our bodies are elsewhere (on the loo, waiting for the bus or — vaguely — playing with or cooking for kids). The promise of apps is much bigger than what they deliver, and it's important that we don't depend on them for more than they can give.

There have been moments when I've enjoyed educating myself via my phone, but real learning happens when I take subjects from my phone and focus on them in a studious way someplace else. Similarly, the promise of connection offered by apps doesn't match up to the real thing. Scrolling through pictures of my friends is more likely to make me envy their lives than it is to make me feel connected to them. There are better ways to use my phone to connect. When I call someone who I care about and ask how they are, it takes me out of my head and I can dive into their world for a moment, or we can come up with an even better plan and meet up later that week for a walk.

Step outside

Walk. Listen to birdsong. Lie down on warm grass and watch the clouds drift by. Pick up a leaf and go find the tree that it fell from. Wrap your arms around that tree and feel it holding you. Stand still. Take your shoes off and walk on the earth. Go outside. Be surprised. Remember that whatever is happening, we can always go outside. We can leave one context and enter something vast and new. The blessing of a new perspective is waiting on the other side of your front door. There is nature, non-human animals and a limitless sky.

I need to go into nature at least once a day. Sometimes I'm too busy and the whole world shrinks to the size of whatever is agitating me. If I can remember to get outside quickly at that moment then I rescue myself from getting lost in my own mind. Instead, I use my body. I walk. I run, stretch, dance and laugh, looking like an idiot in the park near my house.

Rigorous optimism

> We're on the fast track to dystopia and it's going to take a miracle to get us out of there. And that miracle is, of course, collective will.

The Social Dilemma, Netflix documentary

The two questions I try to ask in as many situations as possible are:

'How can I be of service?'

And:

'How can I make this moment better?'

When I ask myself these questions and allow curiosity to discover the answers, life feels meaningful because I have a clear purpose beyond getting my own way. If I participate in communities that ask these questions on a big scale — 'What can we do to be of service? How can we make this moment better?' — then I am working with people to shape a future better than what we have right now.

The hopefulness I feel when I do this work isn't a delusion. I feel better because I belong to something and I see the benefits ripple outwards from the work we do. Looking out for our neighbours makes us feel better. We're nourished by caring for others. In community, we share a hard-won faith that by acting beyond the scope of self-centred gratification, surprising and good things happen. From my own experience, I know this to be true. We do what we do and, by doing it, we generate a psychological air around us; one that is optimistic, compassionate and committed to showing up.

When my perspective is hopeful and I go easily with the flow, my attitude affects other people. I form, and am informed by, the people around me and by the examples of their lives. Our ability to influence other people is a powerful truth. I want to be responsible and kind with that influence.

When we value the power of our influence, our impact becomes less about what we individually achieve and more about how we communally act. Instead of thinking ahead to things we haven't yet achieved or realities that haven't happened, we pay attention to what is happening right now and we bring to that a rigorous belief, borne out in our shared experience, that when we show up for each other things work out.

We build our muscle of optimism by asking what more we can do. We replace guilt and lamenting with connected, positive action, and when we move together, unimaginable realities are within reach.

A letter from your future self

This is the tool that transformed my life. It changed my priorities because it let me see clearly what I wanted more of in my life. It also opened up space for me to think how I would bring these things together in a lasting way. If you haven't paused to take up any of the suggestions I've placed in this book, please do this one. It's a really good gift that you can choose to give yourself.

With a pen and paper in your hand, sitting somewhere quiet and comfortable, imagine yourself at 80 years old. Imagine with specificity what surrounds you and the sort of life you have led. The 80-year-old you that you are imagining was able to live their very best life. Imagine the situation you'd be in, who is nearby and where exactly do you live?

What did you have to do to build this reality and how did you help the world become a place where this imagined 80-year-old — you — could be so fulfilled? Imagine yourself exactly where you hope you will be. Paint with your imagination, fill in all the details — what you had for breakfast, how you spend your days and how you moved from where you are now to being free to build such a beautiful life. What are the things that are major parts of your life? And what have you allowed to fall away?

Now, write a letter as the 80-year-old you to your current self. Thank your present self for all the decisions they made and the paths they took that led you to the seat you are sitting in. Describe the person you have become, the people who surround you, the communities you're a part of and the world that you live upon. Thank the current you for the action they took, between now and then, which made the life you desired happen.

**These are the times
to grow our souls.**

—

Grace Lee Boggs

Afterword:
I promise

We lift our gazes not to what stands between us but what stands before us.

Amanda Gorman, 'The Hill We Climb'

Many years ago, I was part of a protest outside an opencast coal mine in northern Germany. I was living in Berlin and wanted to take part in something that would connect me to the fight against fossil-fuel industries. When I arrived at the protest site, close to the forest that hid the perimeter fence of the mine, I was put in a group with five strangers. We seemed to be the only people who had travelled to the protest alone, so we stuck together as the crowd set off.

We were six people walking amongst hundreds on our way to enter an opencast coal mine. We followed activists chatting in different languages through the quiet of ancient woodland. The forest stretched upwards so we came off the path and scrambled through trees to the top of the hill. When we emerged over the crest and out of the trees we gasped at the harried earth that stretched out to the horizon. The mountain top had been cut off and it hurt to look down at this wound in the earth.

I was still with the new people I'd met. We held the cut fence open and walked down into the mine. For a moment, it felt like we were alone. The mine was so huge that the hundreds of protesters were like ants dropped in tiny groups and lost from one another.

Alongside this group of strangers, the sight of hacked-through earth where nature should have been demanded something more than awkward chitchat. After a conversation, we decided to mark the moment by making a promise to each other. It's a promise I've made hundreds of times with hundreds of people since. Every time I say it, I mean it even more. It's a small ritual that I encourage you to do immediately with someone you love. Once you've spoken it together, I recommend you bring it into your life as a sort of pledge.

To do it you just need these words (or similar words that you can write yourself).

Look into the eyes of the person you're promising and say each line, allowing the person opposite to repeat them back to you. Speak these words aloud right now:

> **I promise**
> **That I will be here**
> **That I will fight for you**
> **For the planet**
> **And for our future**
> **As often as I can.**

We can create a future beyond the limits of our imagination. We can answer our longing and shape the years that come. We can weave ourselves to the power of nature, healing the ways we have been severed from it. We can do all of these things and yet the future will still be the biggest question mark of our time. Our worst fears and most optimistic fantasy won't come close to what reality brings.

Perhaps the infrastructure we have will not hold under climate devastation. Already many systems of governance seem to be creaking at what crises, now and into the future, require of them. More climate impacts will create new pressures on all of us. There will be as many paths forward as there are people on this planet: which is the path that you want to walk along?

We can't do everything, but we can begin to make plans. We choose one or two steps forward and, because we aren't overloaded, we make some progress. Resilience is a foundational principle and it encourages us to become more sophisticated at bringing joy and wonder to the front of our lives.

No one person is going to save the day. The world is too massive and complex for that. Instead, the invitation is there for all of us to be superheroes — the people who, seven generations from now, will be remembered gratefully.

Tread softly now and together be part of nature.

Resources

Read

All About Love: New Visions
— bell hooks

*Braiding Sweetgrass:
Indigenous Wisdom, Scientific
Knowledge and the Teachings
of Plants*
— Robin Wall Kimmerer

*Devotions: The Selected
Poetry of Mary Oliver*
— Mary Oliver

*Emergent Strategy: Shaping
Change, Changing Worlds*
—adrienne maree brown

*Hope in the Dark: Untold
Histories, Wild Possibilities*
— Rebecca Solnit

The Overstory
— Richard Powers

*How We Show Up:
Reclaiming Family, Friendship
and Community*
— Mia Birdsong

The Parable of the Sower
— Octavia E. Butler

The Parable of the Talents
— Octavia E. Butler

*Pleasure Activism:
The Politics of Feeling Good*
— adrienne maree brown

*Wilding: The Return of
Nature to a British Farm*
— Isabella Tree

*Your Silence Will Not Protect
You: Essays and Poems*
— Audre Lorde

Listen

How to Survive the End of the World
A podcast by Autumn Brown
and adrienne maree brown
endoftheworldshow.org

Finding Our Way
A podcast by Prentis Hemphill
prentishemphill.com

Come September
A speech by Arundhati Roy
via YouTube

Follow

@adriennemareebrown
@chicksforclimate
@decolonizeunconference
@earthrise.studio
@futureearth
@heymothership
@intelligentmischief
@mikaelaloach
@ninagualinga
@pattiegonia
@prentishemphill

About the Author

Since dropping banners against Heathrow Airport's third runway from the roof of the Houses of Parliament, Tamsin has consistently shifted public conversation on the climate and ecological emergency.

They have organised (and been arrested for) a number of high-profile protests, co-founded a Suffragette inspired environmental group called Climate Rush, formed a political party 'The Commons', co-ordinated (the successful) Save England's Forests coalition, founded a CIC — The Momentum Project — that mobilises the community surrounding London City Airport, led global corporate campaigns as Head of Global Campaigns at Lush Cosmetics and are a founding member of Extinction Rebellion. They are currently organising with Mothership (@heymothership).

Tamsin is also active in queer uprising, a theatre maker, contributor to *The Book of Queer Prophets* (HarperCollins, 2020) and author of *RUSH! The Making of a Climate Activist* (Marion Boyars, 2009). They are based in London.

Tamsin credits Black feminist organisers for much of the intelligence contained in this book and is therefore donating 50% of their income from *Do Earth* to Black-led community projects that centre around anti-racist and feminist values.

If you'd like to get in touch with Tamsin, please reach out to them on Instagram: *@tamsinomond*

Thanks

I'm grateful to everyone who played a part in making this book. The many teachers I've learnt from, I'm grateful to you all.

Public gratitude to those who made this book possible:

Melissa, my wife, who shows me a world that is light, spacious, trusting and filled with joy.

Miranda who invited this book to exist (and then held it and me so brilliantly as we got it done).

Laetitia whose encouragement got me writing again.

Alice whose photographs have made this book so beautiful.

Shelley my constant Yoda, guide and friend.

Christina and Florence and what we've learnt about unconditional love.

The magic of bookclub's intentional self-educating: Alice, Clare, Fay, Kay and Jo.

Alice HB for companionship.

Jessie, especially this time for introducing me to adrienne maree brown and Mia Birdsong.

Zafira, Nneka and Dani who are chosen family.

Amina who lifts the roof on community organising.

Achala, Alice, Amina, Arizona, Caroline, Christiana, Clare, Daisy, Ed, Fay, Jack and Jenny — in this specific context — for being my first readers and offering gorgeous words of support.

The Lionesses.

The anonymous rooms.

And my family.

Index

'Always Believe' (song) 77
Amelia's Magazine 14
Anderson, Gillian 22
Arctic sea ice 24, 38–9, 42
Attenborough, David 24

banks 51, 59
Berlin 46, 122
BIPOC people (Black, Indigenous, people of colour) 89
Boggs, Grace Lee 118
book clubs 36, 69–71
boundaries, protecting your 84–5
brown, adrienne maree: *Pleasure Activism* 94
Butler, Octavia E.: *Parable of the Sower* 102

Cameron, David 22
Cameron, Julia: *The Artist's Way* 111
campaign, 5 steps to creating an undeniable 91–2
capitalism 28–9, 30, 41, 42, 89–90
charity shops 49
chosen family 68
Clarkson, Jeremy 21
climate change 13, 15, 16, 20, 21, 23, 24, 25, 30, 37, 38, 39–40, 41, 42, 48, 55, 56, 59, 66, 70, 77, 78, 105, 123, 124
Climate Rush 15–16, 17, 21
clothes 49, 59
coal mines 122
coalition government (2010–15) 21
collective action 30, 56, 57–8, 88
community 62–93
community meetings 82–4
consistency 75
COP ('conference of parties') 23–4
courage 55–6
Covid-19 pandemic 68

Dench, Dame Judi 22
denial 39–40
Do Lectures 13, 14, 15, 21

earth 94–110
Ecotricity 50–1
Eddo-Lodge, Reni 70
electronics 49, 59
Emin, Tracy 22
energy, green 50–1
Evening Standard 21

Facebook 79, 90
Fairphone 49
feminism 27, 90
financial crash (2008) 20
food 48
footprint on the earth, softening 30, 46–7, 59
forests, England's public 21–2
fossil-fuels 23, 26, 55, 122
Friends of the Earth 78–9

Gandhi, Mahatma 110
Gichinga, Amina 76–7
Gorman, Amanda: 'The Hill We Climb' 122
Graeber, David 26
Gramsci, Antonio 36; *Prison Notebooks* 36
Grant, John 15
gratitude 81, 110–11
green advertising 15
greenhouse gas emissions 20, 21, 40
Greenpeace 13, 24
Gregory, Amelia 14, 15

Hampstead Heath 98
Haudenosaunee (Iroquois) Great Law of Peace (Gayanashagowa) 103
Heathrow Airport 13, 14, 20, 21
holidays 50–1, 59
hooks, bell 60, 70
Horseferry Road Magistrates' Court 15

Hurricane Sandy 68

Indigenous people 20, 89, 103
individualism 66, 88, 89
Industrial Revolution 37
Institute for Economics and Peace 42
interregnum, the 36–7

Johnson, Rachel 21–2
joy, eco 51
Jumble Trail 81

Lehrer, Riva 89
letter from your future self 117
LGBT people 20–1
London City Airport 22, 75–6, 77, 78
Lorde, Audre 70; *Sister Outsider* 88
Lucas, Caroline 16

Marvel, Dr Kate 38
meat 48, 59
meditation 46, 112–13
Momentum Project, The 76, 77
mushrooms 104–5

National Geographic 103
National Parks 105
Native American 103
Newham 22, 75, 77, 78
Newham Mayor's Show 77
non-violent direct action 14

Obama, Barack 23
Odiete, Ethel 22
Okri, Ben 113
Oliver, Mary: 'Wild Geese' 20
one year off, consumer 49, 59
optimism, rigorous 115–16

Palace of Westminster 16
patriarchy 28, 30, 42, 89
phones
    Fairphone 49
    turning off 113–14
Pride 81
promise ritual 123–4

renewable energy 50–1, 79
resilience 68–9
rewilding 105–7
Royal Docks Singstars 22, 76–8
Royal Festival Hall 77

Save England's Forests 21–2
Section 28 57
Seeds for Change 83
self 32–61
seventh-generation principle 103–4
Shakur, Assata 10
sharing circles 69–71
short-haul flights 50, 59
Sinek, Simon 74
Social Dilemma, The 115
Solnit, Rebecca: *Hope in the Dark* 54
suffragettes 14–15, 21
Sunday Times 14, 15

TedxNewham 22, 77
temperature rise, global 38, 39, 40
Thunberg, Greta 24, 46
transport 49–50, 55, 59, 74
Tree, Isabella: *Wilding* 106–7
trees 26, 59, 96–7, 98–9, 102, 104,
    106, 122

United Nations Framework
    Convention on Climate Change 23
upcycling 49

vegan diet 59

walking 114–15
Westminster Bridge 21
white supremacy 28, 30, 42, 59–60
Winterson, Jeanette: *Why Be Happy
    When You Could Be Normal* 62
writing, daily practice of 111

Yellowstone National Park 105–6

Zen Proverb 112

Books in the series

Do Agile Tim Drake
Do Beekeeping Orren Fox
Do Birth Caroline Flint
Do Bitcoin Angelo Morgan-Somers
Do Breathe
    Michael Townsend Williams
Do Build Alan Moore
Do Deal
    Richard Hoare & Andrew Gummer
Do Death Amanda Blainey
Do Design Alan Moore
Do Disrupt Mark Shayler
Do Drama Lucy Gannon
Do Earth Tamsin Omond
Do Fly Gavin Strange
Do Grow Alice Holden
Do Improvise Robert Poynton
Do Inhabit Sue Fan & Danielle Quigley
Do Lead Les McKeown
Do Listen Bobette Buster

Do Make James Otter
Do Open David Hieatt
Do Pause Robert Poynton
Do Photo Andrew Paynter
Do Present Mark Shayler
Do Preserve
    Anja Dunk, Jen Goss & Mimi Beaven
Do Protect Johnathan Rees
Do Purpose David Hieatt
Do Scale Les McKeown
Do Sea Salt
    Alison, David & Jess Lea-Wilson
Do Sing James Sills
Do Sourdough Andrew Whitley
Do Start Dan Kieran
Do Story Bobette Buster
Do Team Charlie Gladstone
Do Walk Libby DeLana
Do Wild Baking Tom Herbert

Also available

The Book of Do A manual for living edited by Miranda West
Path A short story about reciprocity Louisa Thomsen Brits
The Skimming Stone A short story about courage Dominic Wilcox
Stay Curious How we created a world class event in a cowshed Clare Hieatt
The Path of a Doer A simple tale of how to get things done David Hieatt

Available in print, digital
and audio formats from
booksellers or via our
website: **thedobook.co**

To hear about events and
forthcoming titles, you can find
us on social media **@dobookco**,
or subscribe to our newsletter